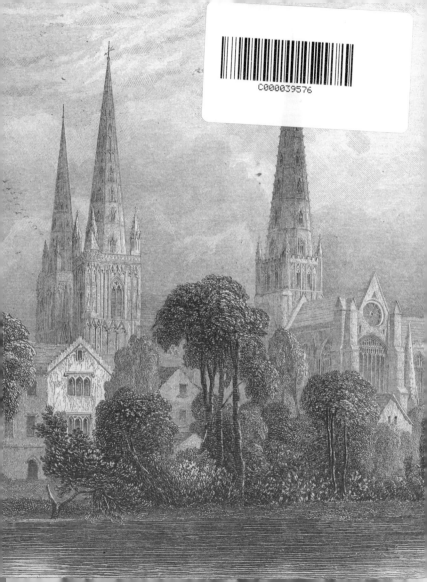

First published 2006 AD
This edition © Wooden Books Ltd 2006 AD

Published by Wooden Books Ltd.
8A Market Place, Glastonbury, Somerset

British Library Cataloguing in Publication Data
Mills, M.
Ancient English Cathedrals

A CIP catalogue record for this book is
available from the British Library

ISBN 1 904263 41 0 ·

Printed and bound in England by
The Cromwell Press, Trowbridge, Wiltshire.
100% recycled papers supplied by Paperback.

ANCIENT ENGLISH
CATHEDRALS

written by

Mark Mills

Dedicated to the Glory of God

Just before the Reformation England had 17 Cathedral Churches of which 9 were old foundation (Chichester, Exeter, Hereford, Lichfield, Lincoln, London St Paul's, Salisbury, Wells and York) and 8 were Monastic Cathedrals (Canterbury, Carlisle, Durham, Ely, Norwich, Rochester, Winchester and Worcester). Henry VIII elevated 6 old Abbey Churches to Cathedrals (Bristol, Chester, Gloucester, Oxford, Peterborough and, briefly, Westminster). Finally, there are 4 further venerable churches of medieval foundation that have been elevated to Cathedral status and appear in this book (St Albans, Southwark, Ripon and Southwell).

Pictures have been taken from various sources, some are from the 1830's series by Winkles, others from 1814-1836 come from Britton's series of volumes, engraved by Mackenzie, Woolnoth and Le Keux. Various others have been taken from 'Our National Cathedrals', Ward Lock & Co 1887.

The front cover shows Wells, the back cover Chester Cloisters. The half-title page shows Litchfield, the title page Salisbury Chapter House and this page Canterbury crypt.

CONTENTS

INTRODUCTION

Where to begin? How can we possibly begin to fathom the intricacies of these great churches? With awe and wonderment! For how else can these great monuments be described? These houses dedicated to the worship of God. Crafted with such skill and devotion that they still stand as a testament to man's ingenuity and faith. Lovingly tended and restored today, history has not always been kind to these great buildings – man and nature have reduced some of these places to virtual ruin, only for them to rise once more from the ashes, making their presence felt and passing their message to all who would stand and listen.

Today we stand in silent admiration at the presence, atmosphere and rare contemplative peace induced by these cathedral churches, but in the past the church was the community's focal point, and when new to a village, town or city the first place one would usually call would be the church. These were places of joy, sorrow, inspiration and learning, places of song and reverence, reflecting the ingenuity and work of numerous generations of stone masons, artists, craftsmen and architects that worked for the greater glory of God. Embodying the timeless principles of geometry, harmony and cosmology, from the finest details to the most monumental structural forms that support roofs, ribbed vaulting and towers, stained glass, woodwork, sculpture and ironwork, the cathedral brings all together to truly evoke a feeling of the divine.

Their chequered histories lead us along paths of discovery that are as inspirational as the buildings themselves. Some have histories that predate their current construction, sited on Saxon churches built on Roman sites, themselves sited on earlier holy places.

None of our existing cathedrals have survived from Saxon times except in certain circumstances where occasional elements predate the Norman period. After the Norman Conquest to the end of the twelfth century we find what can be classed as the first great period of cathedral building. William the Conqueror brought with him great change, Sees were moved to larger cities and Norman bishops were placed in most of the dioceses. Monastic communities were formed in many cathedrals under Benedictine rule, Ripon was Augustine, and the remaining cathedrals that were run by clergy who would not take monastic vows were classed as secular.

The Norman period is characterised by a distinctly Roman influence with round pillars, flat ceilings, distinctive rounded arches and undivided windows. Ornamentation is mainly rounds and hollows, chevrons and zigzag lines. Columns start as massive structural forms, developing into multi-angular shapes, later formed as a thick central core surrounded by three-quarter columns. Deeply recessed doorways were flanked by slender receding columns on either side. Predominantly based on a Latin Cross plan the west end was the main entrance with North and South transepts and a semicircular apse. Low towers came into existence at the west end, and in later Norman churches a tall tower was introduced at the crossing.

By the end of the twelfth century, during the reign of Henry II, a new era of architecture was established, the Early English, or Gothic. The high pitched roofs of this style and the characteristic pointed arch and vaulting set it apart from the earlier Norman work. Windows are elongated and lancet in shape, with circlets, triplets and trefoils positioned above the lancet and within the outer arch. Foliage was introduced into the ornamentation along with dogtooth sculpture, doors are pointed and often double. Towers rose to greater heights and were further extended by the addition of spires, Salisbury Cathedral stands as probably the finest example of the this period.

In the late thirteenth early fourteenth century the Decorated style established itself, with striking ornamentation in doorways, windows, pinnacles and roofs. Instead of separate lancets, windows were combined, with light stone mullions or dividing pillars becoming intrinsic, and elaborate tracery replacing the simpler patterns of the Early English. Doorways of this period are less deeply recessed with arches decorated by flower mouldings. Beautifully carved and embellished niches were created for statuary, and spires elaborately decorated. A great part of Exeter and Lichfield Cathedrals belong to this period.

The end of the fourteenth century ushered in the perpendicular style, continuing until the middle of the sixteenth century. The period is charac-terised by lower arches, square tops placed over doorways and strikingly vertical window mullions, often with strong cross subdivisions. Bands and mouldings on pillars became shallow, and panelling and fan tracery prevailed as did the Tudor flower and angel.

There followed the ecclesiastical destruction performed by Henry VIII and during the Reformation which was so methodical and widespread that for fear of tedious and depressing effect little mention will be made of it in these pages. Many of the cathedrals in this book were of course established by Henry the year after he had dissolved their monasteries.

With the Renaissance classical models again became fashionable, producing St Pauls, one of the finest examples of this period. Finally, the extensive restoration of many cathedrals which took place in successive centuries, notably in the mid 1800s by Sir George Gilbert Scott, was followed by the modern period which ushered in completely new styles and forms.

Space is limited here, so I hope the reader will forgive the condensed style and numerous omissions, and quietly enjoy the extraordinary stories of these magnificent buildings, celebrations in stone of the divine.

BRISTOL

Cathedral Church of the Holy & Undivided Trinity

Founded in 1140 as an Augustinian abbey, building commenced immediately on this great Norman church, and in the successive centuries further building and rebuilding was undertaken with equal vigour. Archaeological evidence suggests that a religious house was on this site before the Augustinians arrived but no historical records exist to support this.

Some of the original Norman work still survives, particularly the Chapter House and Abbey Gatehouse. The cathedral peculiarly has two lady chapels, the early 13th century 'elder' Lady Chapel, and the 14th century Eastern Lady Chapel. The interior of the cathedral is spectacular and surpasses any work of its time in Europe. The chancel vault is the earliest lierne vault in England, and Bristol uniquely displays a nave, choir and aisles all with the same height, making it one of the finest examples of a hall church in the world.

The abbey was dissolved in 1539 and the incomplete nave partially demolished before it was elevated to a diocese in 1542, becoming a cathedral by decree of Henry VIII. In the 15th Century the rebuilding of the transepts and the main tower began but it was not until the 19th century that building work was finally completed under Abbot Knowle with the architect G.E. Street. The nave was finally opened in 1877 and the towers in 1888.

CANTERBURY

Christ Church

The first seat of episcopal power in Britain, Canterbury began its life as a church, given by King Ethelbert of Kent and his Christian wife Queen Bertha to St Augustine when he arrived in Britain in 597 with a group of 40 monks, sent by Pope Gregory to convert the locals. St Augustine soon established his seat ('See' or 'cathedra') as the first Archbishop of Canterbury. A Benedictine monastic community was thriving by the 10th century.

The original cathedral church suffered misfortune and ruin, finally burning to the ground in 1067 only to be rebuilt shortly afterwards by Lanfranc, Abbot of Caen. An architect, Lanfranc started from scratch and the resulting Romanesque cathedral church was dedicated to Jesus Christ in 1114 AD.

Thomas Becket, appointed archbishop by his friend Henry II, was famously murdered in the cathedral in 1170 by four rogue knights for placing his service to God above his duty to the King. Proclaimed a martyr and canonised in 1173, Becket's popular shrine was destroyed by Henry VIII in 1538.

In 1174 the choir burned down and was rebuilt over the next nine years, creating an inspiring Gothic precedent built mostly in Purbeck marble. A new nave was completed in 1405. The monastery was dissolved by Henry VIII in 1540, and the cathedral sacked in 1642 by the puritans only to be completely repaired and refurbished before the end of the 17th century.

CARLISLE

Cathedral Church of the Holy & Undivided Trinity

Carlisle is uniquely situated on an ancient battle line. The Romans built a wall through it and the English and Scots fought over it for over 500 years.

In 685 St Cuthbert visited the site prior to his death on Holy Island a few years later, and in 875 the city was destroyed by Vikings. In 1092 a new church was founded by Walter, a Norman priest appointed by William II as governor of Carlisle. The new church was completed in 1125 by Henry I and converted into a priory of Augustinian canons five years later. In 1133 it was made the See of a diocese embracing Cumberland and North Westmoreland, becoming the sole episcopal chapter of the Augustinian Order in England, the only Augustinian priory to be elevated to cathedral status.

Stone supposedly gathered from Hadrian's Wall during its construction in the 12th century to build the nave was later removed by the Scots between 1645 and 1652 for defensive walls whilst Carlisle was under siege. The cathedral stands today with only two bays of its original eight in nave.

In 1660 restoration work began which has continued ever since, creating a lovingly cared-for building which has survived some of the most destructive history to be directed against any cathedral. 14th century detail remains in the east window tracery and glass, and the painted ceiling in the choir.

CHESTER

Cathedral Church of Christ & the Blessed Virgin Mary

Originally founded by the Romans as a station for one of their legions, Chester became home in 907 to the remains of St Werburgh, a Mercian princess who had become a nun, and later an abbess. Her new home was an early Saxon minster which in 1092 was rebuilt by the colourful Hugh Lupus Earl of Chester. He expelled the secular order and settled there an abbot and an order of Benedictine monks, who promptly rebuilt the church and turned it into the centrepiece of the Abbey of St Werburgh.

In 1250 the heavy Norman church began to be transformed into a larger lighter and more elegant Gothic building. The new medieval church, the cathedral we see today, was put up over the Norman church, the earlier version being slowly taken down from the inside.

The abbey was dissolved by King Henry VIII in 1540, and restored by him the following year as the seat of a bishop. Upon becoming a See the church was dedicated to Christ and the blessed Virgin Mary, and refounded for a dean, 6 prebendaries, 6 minor canons, a deacon, 6 singing men, 6 choristers, 2 masters of grammar, 24 scholars, 6 almsmen, a verger, 2 sextons, 2 porters of which one a barber and one a cook, one undercook, etc ...

Having been neglected in the following centuries, the cathedral was extensively restored by Sir George Gilbert Scott in the late 19th century.

CHICHESTER

Cathedral of the Holy Trinity

Originally established by St Wilfred on the Isle of Selsey in 681 the See of the South Saxons was removed north to Chichester in 1075 by the Conqueror and his bishop, Stigand. Of the old cathedral at Selsey nothing now remains, though it is said that its bells can still be heard at low tide under the ocean.

Stigand designed and laid the foundations for the new cathedral before he died, and the cathedral was finally consecrated by Bishop Luffa in 1108.

Remarkably preserved this cathedral has kept most of its original Norman structure, the only noticeable difference being the extension of the Lady Chapel, and to a degree the rebuilding of the nave's western bays by Henry I following a fire in 1114, and work following another fire in 1187.

Chapels were added to the nave aisles in the 13th century, giving Chichester its great width. Other additions followed in the 14th and 15th centuries.

On 21st February 1861 the central tower collapsed, concertinaing itself into a pile of rubble and timbers in the centre of the cathedral. A new tower was immediately planned by Gilbert Scott, started in 1865 and completed the following year. The 277 ft spire echoed the old one, the only spire visible from the sea and used as a landmark by mariners for hundreds of years.

DURHAM

Cathedral Church of Christ & the Blessed Virgin Mary

Standing on a mass of rock, with the River Wear snaking around its base in a horseshoe, Durham Cathedral stands as a testament to the ingenuity of medieval craftsmen. It is the least altered of our cathedrals and was the first in England to have ribbed vaults of stone over the whole space.

The site is associated with St Cuthbert, 7th century Bishop of Lindisfarne, whose remains were a treasured possession of the monastery on Holy Island. Attacked by Vikings in 875, the monks fled to the mainland and finally settled in Durham in 995, there building a church to house the saintly remains.

After the Norman Conquest in 1080 the Earl Bishop William St Carileph refounded Durham as a cathedral priory, and in 1093 began rebuilding the church using Norman designs. It was completed in 1135 after his death.

With its cruciform plan except for the eastern end of the choir and the central tower this is a wholly Norman building, the emphasis being placed on the height and rhythm of the arcade. The piers having been further embellished with zig-zags, lozenges, spirals and flutes create a most dramatic first impression. The pointed diamond ribbed vaulting is the earliest in Europe, as are the flying buttresses, cunningly invented and hidden in the triforium by the Norman masons working at Durham.

ELY

Cathedral Church of the Holy Trinity

Originally an island in the vast marshy Norfolk fens, Ely was given to the Saxon princess St Etheldreda by her first husband. On her release from her marriage vows to a second husband, and still a virgin, she fled to Ely and in 673 founded a double monastery for monks and nuns on the site of the present cathedral. She became the first abbess of her own foundation, and Ely was guided by successive abbesses until sacked by the Vikings in 870.

The Isle was occupied by a college of secular priests until the reign of King Edgar when it was again attacked by the Vikings before being reconsecrated as a Benedictine community by Ethelwold Bishop of Winchester in 970. A site of considerable importance in Saxon times, Ely ranked as powerfully as Canterbury and Glastonbury. During the Norman Conquest Thurston was abbot and defended the Isle against William for 7 years.

In 1083 Abbot Simeon commenced work on a new building very close to the original Saxon church, and the remains of St. Etheldreda were moved to the choir in 1106. Ely was elevated to a cathedral in 1109.

Today the original Norman transepts and nave still stand, but a 14th century collapse of the crossing tower resulted in the construction of Ely's exquisite octagonal lantern. The labyrinth was designed by Gilbert Scott in 1870.

EXETER

Cathedral Church of St Peter

Built on a Roman camp, the Abbey Church of St. Peter was founded in 939 by monks of the Benedictine order beside an earlier Christian structure possibly dating back as early as the 5th century. Progress was slow, the monks having to flee bloodthirsty Vikings on a number of occasions. They were coaxed back by King Edgar in 968, and again by Canute in 1019.

When Leofric became Bishop of the See in 1046 he immediately set about moving it from Crediton to the walled town of Exeter, and the old minster became the new cathedral church. His successor, Bishop Warelwast, laid the foundation stone of the cathedral we know today in 1112.

The only visible remaining parts of his cathedral today are the two transept towers, after successive Bishops and building projects transformed the cathedral over the next 200 years, adding a chapter house in the Decorated Gothic style, and other buildings and halls around the cathedral close.

Fortunately for the cathedral it survived the Second World War despite a direct hit on 3 May 1942 and Exeter being nearly leveled. With its vaulting intact and the whole cathedral lovingly cared for and restored this magnificent cathedral can be enjoyed for generations to come.

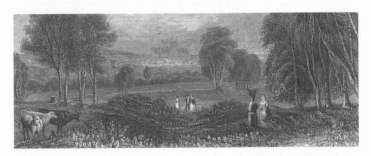

GLOUCESTER

Cathedral Church of St Peter & the Holy and Indivisible Trinity

---

In AD 49 the Romans entered 'Caer Glow', forming a fortress there, and by 189 Gloucester is reputed to have had a Christian community. The Roman garrison withdrew in 410, and we know Gloucester had a Bishop by 490.

In 679 the Saxon King Osric founded the monastery of St Peter, presided over by its first abbess, his sister Kyneburga. Later, King Bernulph appointed secular canons to Gloucester in 823, these being eventually removed by King Canute in 1017 to make way for Benedictine monks.

By 1072, when William's first chaplain Serlo succeeded Abbot Wilstan, the monastery was down to just 2 monks and 8 novices. An entire rebuilding of the church and monastery was commenced on 29 June 1089. Completed in 1120, a fire two years later caused extensive damage to the nave, not repaired until 1242 when a new vault over the nave was finished. The 14th century saw the perpendicular remodelling of the Quire and the building of the Great Cloister, whilst the tower and Lady Chapel both date to the 15th century.

One of the most striking features of this great church is the three-storied design. Much of the original Norman work is still visible under the later renovations and modifications, and follows a classic basilican effect with a long unbroken range of columns, producing a feeling of great height.

HEREFORD

Cathedral Church of the Blessed Virgin Mary and St Ethelbert

In Saxon times Hereford was situated in part of Mercia. It may have been the site of a See as early as 544, with an archbishop residing at St Davids. In 794 Ethelbert, the young king of the East Angles, arrived in Mercia to marry King Offas's daughter, but was instead murdered on his orders, and later canonised, with a cathedral church being built in 825 to house the remains.

The church was rebuilt by Bishop Athelstan around 1030, only to be destroyed shortly afterwards by a Welsh army, so when Robert de Losinga took over the See in 1079 he was faced with the task of rebuilding the ruined Saxon church. The Norman cathedral we see today was largely built in the first half of the 12th century, with Gothic additions over the next 200 years.

On Easter Monday in 1786 the west tower collapsed, destroying the entire west end. Restoration work by James Wyatt resulted in little but the piers and arches remaining from the 12th century. The piers themselves are massive cylinders with richly carved capitals executed with a degree of refinement typical of late Norman work. The crossing tower remained intact. Built from a greyish pink sandstone from Hollington, the cathedral has a total length now of 360 feet and houses the Mappa Mundi and Chained Library.

LICHFIELD

Cathedral Church of the Blessed Virgin Mary and St Chad

When Chad was made Bishop of Mercia in 669 he moved the See from Repton to Lichfield, the centre of the Saxon kingdom, and possibly a Christian site as early as 300. After Chad's death a cathedral church was consecrated by Bishop Hedda in 700 to house his bones. In 785 Lichfield was briefly exalted to an archbishopric by King Offa with papal approval, but under his successor Kenulph rights and privileges were soon returned to Canterbury.

In 1085 work began to replace the Saxon church with a Norman cathedral, which itself was soon slowly replaced by a Gothic cathedral.

During the Civil War Lichfield suffered terribly, not only was it garrisoned, it was fortified and laid siege to by each side during the conflict. The centre spire was battered down in 1646 and the roof demolished by 1660; glasswork, statues and monuments were destroyed, mutilated and defaced.

Restoration work was started under Bishop John Hackett in 1661, a work of passion financed almost entirely from his own funds. William Wyatt made changes to the ordering in the 18th century, and Gilbert Scott further restored the cathedral's splendour in the late 19th century.

Lichfield's three spires are called the Ladies of the Vale. Made of stone, the centre spire stands 258 ft and the western spires about 200 ft.

LINCOLN

Cathedral Church of the Blessed Virgin Mary

Apart from Durham no other English cathedral is so dominantly placed as that of Lincoln. In the 1st century the Romans built a fortress and then a town on top of the hill, and in the 7th century in the former forum in the heart of the town we find the first Christian church.

In 1072, following a decision by the Conqueror to move Sees to fortified towns, Bishop Remigus moved from Dorchester to Lincoln and began building a new cathedral. Following a fire 1141, the cathedral was restored by Bishop Alexander, this time using stone vaulting for the roof instead of wood, and adding new stages to the western towers. The original stark western front so characteristic of early Norman workmanship was revived with intersecting arches, ornamental portals and a frieze of unique relief sculptures.

But bad luck struck again, as on Palm Sunday 1185 an earthquake devastated all but the west front and twin towers. The Bishop at the time was St Hugh, from Avalon near Grenoble, who soon supervised the magnificent building from the rubble of one of the very first true Gothic cathedrals.

The collapse of the central tower in 1237 resulted in further enlargements and improvements and the Angel choir was consecrated in 1280. Further stages were added to the towers in the 14th century, and by 1549, when it blew down, the spire on the central tower was the highest in Britain.

NORWICH

Cathedral Church of the Holy and Undivided Trinity

The diocese of Norwich is one of the most ancient in England, the See having been founded in 630 in Dunwich, capital of the East Angles, by St Felix. Later the See moved to Thetford and then onto Norwich in 1095.

Herbert de Losinga Bishop of East Anglia immediately embarked upon a grand building project which would see the rise of Norwich cathedral and an attached priory of Benedictine monks on the site. His first course of action was the compulsory purchasing of a large part of the town, followed swiftly by the ruthless leveling of the houses in question to make way for his vision.

No Anglo-Norman cathedral has been altered less than Norwich; the cathedral has never had a saint's shrine, and so has never needed any extending or remodeling. Neither a fire in 1171, nor riots between angry townsfolk and monks in 1272, nor the 1363 destruction of the spire in a storm or even the burning of the replacement spire by lightning in 1463 caused any lasting damage to the cathedral. The final 315 feet replacement spire was built in 1480 with brick and faced in stone. Some restoration was started in 1660 followed serious vandalism during the Civil War.

Look out for the 1,106 carved roof bosses, each with its own rich story.

OXFORD

The Cathedral Church of Christ

The smallest cathedral in England, Oxford began as a nunnery founded in the 8th century by St Frideswide, the pious daughter of King Didan and Safrida who fled to Oxford to escape the advances of the Mercian King Algar. Burnt to the ground in 1002 by Vikings, it was refounded as an Augustinian priory in 1122, and parts of the chapter house date back to this time.

Work started on the cathedral church of today in 1160; the design is late Romanesque, with large round pillars and exquisite capitals, and in 1180 the shrine of St Frideswide was installed in its special chapel.

In 1525 the priory and numerous other religious houses were dissolved by Cardinal Wolsey to make room for his vision for Cardinal's College. The western half of the nave was demolished to make way for the base court, a great hall and kitchen were built to the south of the court and to the north a large chapel was laid out to replace the existing St Frideswides. Fortunately Wolsey fell from favour in 1529 and work ceased.

Henry VIII refounded the college twice, first as Henry VIII's college in 1532, and then as Christ Church College in 1546 with a Dean and 8 canons. He transferred the See from nearby Oseney to St Frideswides, enabling him to acquire Oseney Abbey and its estates.

PETERBOROUGH

Cathedral Church of St Peter, St Paul and St Anthony

The first church at Peterborough was part of an abbey founded in 655 by King Peada of Mercia which was razed by Vikings in 870 and refounded as a Benedictine community in the tenth century by King Edgar.

The church was the only part of the abbey to survive Hereward the Wake's resistance to the Norman Conquest in 1069, finally burning down in 1116 in a great fire. Two years later work began on the present building.

Having completed the transepts and the nave in perfect Romanesque Norman style the masons began adopting the fashionable Gothic look which was then in its early stages and already creating irreversible changes to the way things were designed. The magnificent western front which was added in the 13th century is completely Gothic. Don't miss the original 13th century wooden ceiling, the only one in the country, and one of only four ceilings of this period surviving in the whole of Europe.

The church was not elevated to cathedral status until 1541.

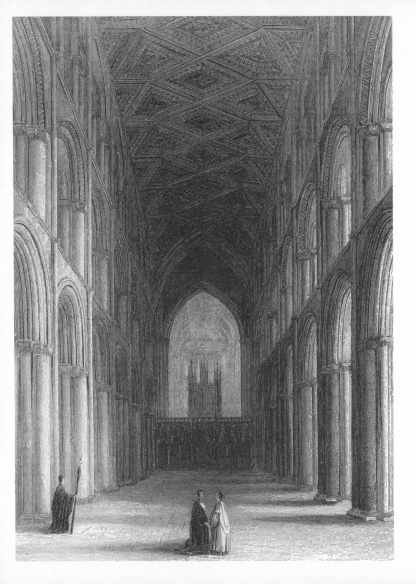

RIPON

Cathedral Church of St Peter and St Wilfred

In 1836 Ripon Minster became a cathedral, elevated by the creation of a new diocese. However, its history extends well before the Norman Conquest, Scottish monks establishing the first church on the site in 660.

In 672 Wilfred became abbot, changing the rule from Scottish to Benedictine, and relocating and rebuilding the monastery on a different site. The crypt is the only part of St Wilfred's magnificent church to survive after the complex was razed by the Crown in 948 as a warning to the Archbishop of York. It became a collegiate and the church a mere parish church.

A complete rebuild was begun in 1154 by Archbishop Roger Pont l'Evêque, followed in 1230 by the construction of twin towers at the nave's west end, and at the end of the 13th century, following a collapse, the rebuilding of the east end of the church. Further building work was needed when part of the crossing tower collapsed in 1450, and during the reign of Henry VIII the nave was completely rebuilt to include aisles, completed in 1528.

In the 17th century the wood and lead spires that had topped the towers were removed following the collapse of the central spire through the roof. Restoration work from 1862-70 was under the direction of Gilbert Scott.

ROCHESTER

Cathedral Church of Christ and the Blessed Virgin Mary

This ancient and undisturbed diocese was founded in 604 by Bishop Justus, on the orders of St Augustine, but by the time of the Conquest the cathedral was in a poor state of repair having been repeatedly sacked by Vikings.

In 1082 a Benedictine priory was established under the guiding hand of the Norman Bishop Gundulf and work started on a new nave the following year. Building work continued rapidly for Gundulf was a master stonemason and on Ascension Day 1130 the cathedral was consecrated in the presence of Henry I. A fire in 1137 caused considerable damage but allowed a Gothic rebuild of the quire and ceiling. In 1215 the cathedral was plundered by King John, holding it against the rebel barons, and it was later desecrated by Simon de Montfort's troops when they captured the city.

Throughout the next 300 years building continued, particularly in the Quire, north and south transepts and Lady Chapel, only ceasing when funds ran short. Still in place from the time of construction Rochester now has the oldest choir stalls in England, the back stalls dating back to 1227.

Continual restoration work has taken place over the centuries. In 1825 the crossing tower and spire were demolished, eventually reopening in 1904.

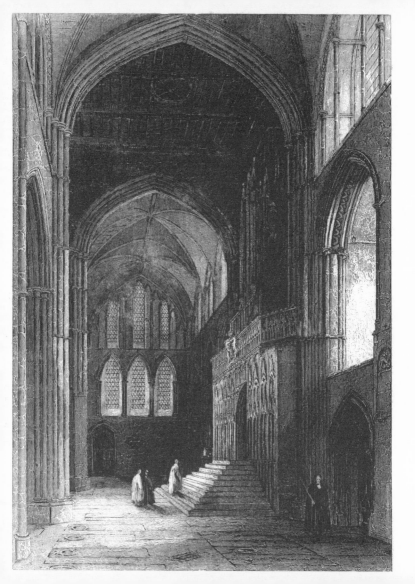

SALISBURY

Cathedral Church of the Blessed Virgin Mary

Salisbury is the only English cathedral built on a fresh site in the Gothic period. In 1217 Bishop Richard Poore got permission to move the site of the late 11th century Norman cathedral a few miles south from the impressive Iron Age hill fort of Old Sarum to a new site beside the River Avon.

Founded in 1220 the new cathedral took 38 years to finish and from the very beginning was planned on a magnificent scale and laid out in its entirety on the site. It is one of the only cathedrals completed in accordance with its original design, and subsequently contains the purest Early English work.

The walls and buttresses are of local Chilmark stone and the cylindrical shafts of the pillars and other elements are of Purbeck marble. The main addition to the cathedral since its completion is the 180 ft crossing tower spire, started in 1300, with its pinnacle 404 ft above the ground. Remarkable in its design for purity, simplicity and grandeur, this cathedral exemplifies the beautiful pointed style.

Over the centuries the tower and spire have been made safe in every respect including the addition of iron ties in the lantern story of the tower. The tower's declination was tested by use of a plumb line to see if any of the towers legs had settled - a method still used today.

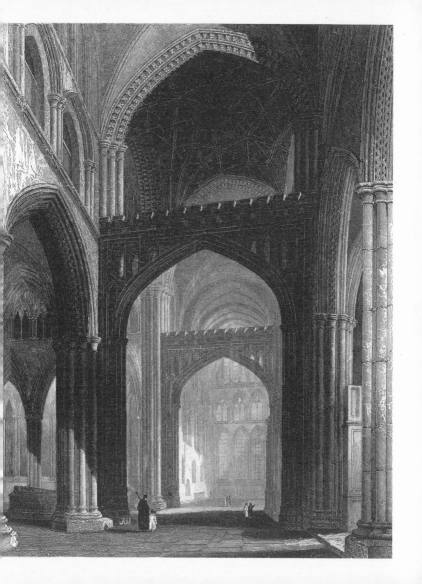

SOUTHWARK

Cathedral & Collegiate Church of St Saviour & St Mary Overie

This ancient church was reputedly founded in the early ninth century by a house of Sisters to maintain a ferry across the Thames, "over-the-rie" meaning "over-the-water". In 852 the parish church of St Mary's was changed into a collegiate church and a house of Augustinian canons was established by the bishop of Winchester, then St Swithin.

In 1106 the church was rebuilt by the bishop of Winchester and its foundation changed to that of a monastery. Destroyed by fire in 1206 it was promptly again rebuilt by the bishop of Winchester and completed by 1230. Later additions include the 150 ft tower completed in circa 1520.

Three centuries of neglect, decay, fire and sporadic building work left the church in a poor state. The nave roof collapsed in 1468 and a lighter oak roof replaced it. The church narrowly avoided demolition to make way for London Bridge and a new nave was built following its collapse in 1838.

Finally in the 19th century Sir Arthur Bloomfield directed extensive restoration and building which was sympathetic to the church, harmonizing its appearance to the Early English style. In 1897 the church re-opened as a collegiate church, in 1904 an Act of Parliament created the diocese of Southwark and in 1905 the church was elevated to a cathedral.

The Globe Theatre   St. Saviour's Church

Shakespeare's Southwark

SOUTHWELL

Cathedral Church of the Blessed Virgin Mary

Knowledge of the early history of Southwell is patchy. A Roman Christian font found nearby indicates that Christianity was flourishing in the area prior to 410. We know that Paulinus, Archbishop of York, was baptising believers in the River Trent in 627, and legend tells that he founded a church.

In 956 King Eadwig gave land in Southwell to Oskytel Archbishop of York, founding a Saxon collegiate minster church for secular canons. Then in 1108 a great Norman church took its place, as part of a rebuilding project by Thomas II, Archbishop of York. As an incentive in his appeal for help he released parishioners from having to visit the church of York each year, and bestowed the same status upon the church of St. Mary's of Southwell.

Of the original Norman building work more than half is still in place, the nave is predominantly Norman, although the lack of vaulting shafts and the use of strong horizontal string courses create an emphasis that is more horizontal than vertical. The original Quire was completely rebuilt in the thirteenth century by Walter de Gray, Archbishop of York, who replaced it in the Early English Gothic style between 1234 and 1241. White Mansfield sandstone is used throughout, its fine grain lending itself especially to interior work.

Considered for cathedral status by Henry VIII, it was not until 1884 that Southwell was elevated to a cathedral.

ST ALBANS

Cathedral and Abbey Church of St Alban

This abbey church was founded by King Offa of Mercia in 730 to commemorate the site of the martyrdom of Alban, a citizen of Verulamium and the first man in Britain to die for the Christian faith, around 250.

From 1066 to 1077 the monastery suffered terribly at the hands of William I, and would have been utterly destroyed had not Lanfranc intervened. Shortly after the completion of Canterbury a Benedictine monk, Paul of Caen, was made abbot in 1077. He promptly brought over from Normandy a band of masons, who set about demolishing the existing Saxon church and replacing it with a 380 foot long Norman church. Roman bricks acquired from the ruins of the nearby Roman city of Verulamium were used in the construction of the central tower, walls and piers. In the early 13th century the site was one of the most important Benedictine houses in the country.

When the abbey was dissolved in 1539 it once again suffered dreadfully with numerous monastic buildings being destroyed. We can still see much of the original work, however, as the transepts, central tower and parts of the nave have survived the rigours of time and restoration.

ST PAUL'S

Cathedral Church of St Paul

The see of London was established as early as 314 and in 604 a Saxon cathedral was founded on the current site. Destroyed by Vikings it was rebuilt in 962, only to be burned, along with much of the city, by the fire of 1083. It was not until 1315 that the magnificent Norman replacement, known today as 'Old St Paul's', was finished, a great cathedral with the longest nave and chancel in Europe and, at 489 ft, the tallest spire in Europe too.

Fire struck again. In 1666 during the Great Fire of London the cathedral suffered irreparable damage. The ruins of Old St. Paul's were cleared and on 21st June 1675 Sir Christopher Wren laid the first stone of the cathedral we see today, finished 35 years later by his son who laid the last and highest stone on top of the lantern. Built of fine Portland stone the plan of the cathedral is that of a Latin cross. It has a twin-towered western front and a featured crossing. Eight enormous pillars support the 68,000 tons of downward force that span the crossing which is covered with a magnificent dome, beneath which the famous Whispering Gallery may be found.

Wren was reputed to have found in the ruins of the old burnt out cathedral a shattered stone slab bearing the single word *resurgam*, 'I shall rise again'. In response to this tiding of good fortune a phoenix rising from ashes is displayed above the entrance to the south transept.

WELLS

Cathedral Church of St Andrew

Permission to found an Anglo-Saxon church beside the great spring at Wells is believed to have originated with King Ine of Wessex in 705; and in 766 the church is documented in a charter. It was elevated to a cathedral in 909 when the diocese of Sherborne was divided.

After the Norman Conquest the See was moved to Bath, and Wells became the church of a college of secular canons until once more elevated to a cathedral in 1244. Building work had begun in 1176 under Bishop Reginald, and under Bishop Jocelyn (1206-42) a grand Bishop's Palace was also built south of the cathedral. Spectacular scissor arches were installed in the crossing in 1338 after structural weaknesses in the central tower became apparent. A 14th century timber and lead spire burnt down in 1439.

Wells is the earliest completely Gothic cathedral in Europe and has a very English character with no French influence, especially its incredible west front which is still adorned with nearly 300 medieval carved figures. A distinctive feature of this cathedral is the triplication of all shafts, even where single shafts would normally have been used.

WINCHESTER

Cathedral Church of the Holy Trinity, St Peter & Paul, & St Swithin

---

A cathedral was first built on this site in 634, and the plan of that ancient building is still marked outside to the north of the present nave. Bishop of Winchester from 852-62 was Swithin, the trusted counsellor of Egbert, King of the West Saxons. Egbert was grandfather to Alfred the Great who was to push back the Vikings and unify the kingdom of Wessex with Winchester at its heart. In the 10th century it became a Benedictine priory and Swithin was canonised after miraculous cures took place at his shrine. It is said that the weather on his feast day (July 15th) sets the weather for the next 40 days.

The present cathedral was started in 1079 in the Romanesque style and was immediately designed to be massive. Today only the original crypt and transepts survive. In 1107 the crossing tower fell, the east end was extended in the 13th century, and the western towers were demolished in the 14th century, troubled by ongoing problems of stability. The nave was extensively remodelled around 1400 and other building work continued.

From 1906 to 1911 diver William Walker, working in water up to 20 feet deep shored up the southern and eastern sides with 25,000 bags of concrete, 115,000 concrete blocks and 900,000 bricks. He was awarded the MVO.

WORCESTER

Cathedral Church of Christ and the Blessed Virgin Mary

Nestled against the River Severn, the site was settled in the Iron Age, then occupied by the Romans and Saxons. Around 679 the diocese encompassing Mercia was divided up by Archbishop Theodore of Canterbury to create new Bishoprics for the various tribes and subkingdoms, and the church of St Peter was established with a chapter of secular clerks.

In 961 Oswald was appointed bishop and established in 983 a new church and Benedictine order dedicated to St Mary, transferring St Peter's powers to St Mary's which became Worcester Cathedral, but the new building was soon burned and plundered by Vikings in 1041.

The Saxon bishop Wulstan of Worcester 1062-95 was the only prelate in the country not to be replaced by Norman ecclesiastics. Deploring the Norman habit of tearing down Saxon churches and replacing them with new buildings, he began to rebuild St Mary's himself, paying special attention to the crypt that was to contain the remains of St Oswald. A fire in 1113 slowed building work, however, and it was not until 1170 that the nave was completed in the newer transitional style. Building work continued until the late 14th century, with the cloisters eventually being completed in the 1432.

Despite enthusiastic restoration work carried out in the 18th and 19th centuries Worcester's architecture and interior are exquisite.

YORK

Cathedral Church of St Peter

The site of a Roman fortress, York had its own bishop by 314. In 627 the newly converted King Edwin of Northumbria built a small wooden minster, soon rebuilt in stone by his successor St Oswald, and restored by his successor St Wilfred. York was overrun with pagan Vikings throughout the late 9th and 10th centuries, and by 1066 it was a Danish archbishop, Ealred, who travelled south from York to anoint and crown William the Conqueror.

The first Norman archbishop Thomas of Bayeux immediately began to rebuild the old church in 1070 but the Vikings repeatedly attacked and in 1080 he decided to construct a new 365 ft long cathedral church. Then, in 1220 Archbishop Walter de Gray decided to rebuild the entire minster, a project that lasted until 1475 and embraced the various styles of the day.

The crossing tower spire collapsed in 1407 and Henry IV sent his own master mason to oversee repairs to the masonry and strengthen the piers, but York continued to suffer from unstable foundations and it was not until 1972 that the problem was final put to rest through extensive underpinning.

The east window is the largest medieval painted glass window in Europe.

CATHEDRAL GROUND PLANS

from Bannister Fletcher's History of Architecture 1895

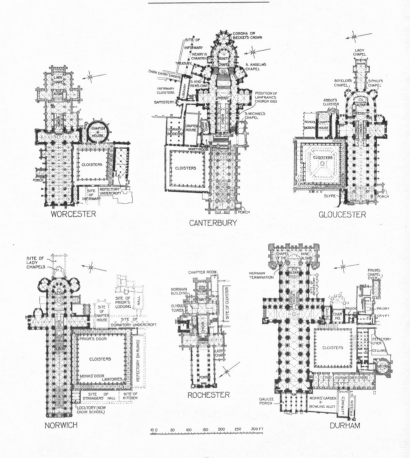

WORCESTER

CANTERBURY

GLOUCESTER

NORWICH

ROCHESTER

DURHAM

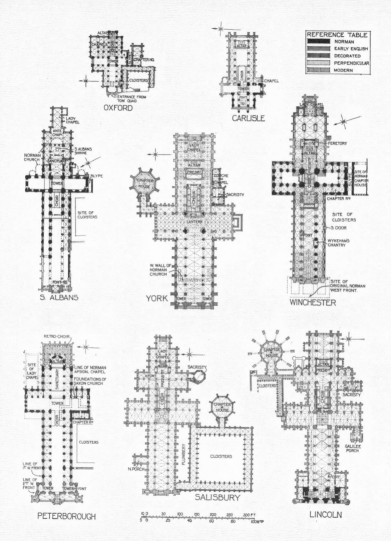

REFERENCE TABLE
NORMAN
EARLY ENGLISH
DECORATED
PERPENDICULAR
MODERN

OXFORD

CARLISLE

S. ALBANS

YORK

WINCHESTER

PETERBOROUGH

SALISBURY

LINCOLN

57

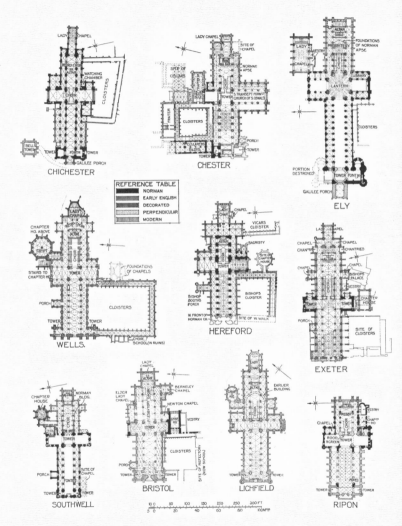

CHICHESTER

CHESTER

ELY

REFERENCE TABLE
NORMAN
EARLY ENGLISH
DECORATED
PERPENDICULAR
MODERN

WELLS.

HEREFORD

EXETER

SOUTHWELL

BRISTOL

LICHFIELD

RIPON